A Woman Of Value

A BIBLE STUDY FOR WOMEN

A Woman Of
VALUE

10 Studies from Proverbs

Dee Brestin

ChariotVICTOR
PUBLISHING
A DIVISION OF COOK COMMUNICATIONS

Titles by Dee Brestin

From Victor Books

The Friendships of Women

The Friendships of Women Workbook

We Are Sisters

The Joy of Hospitality: A Bible Study Guide for Women

The Joy of Women's Friendships: A Bible Study Guide for Women

The Joy of Eating Right: A Bible Study Guide for Women

A Woman of Joy

A Woman of Value

A Woman of Insight

Fisherman Bible Study Guides

(HAROLD SHAW PUBLISHERS)

Proverbs and Parables

Examining the Claims of Christ (John 1-5)

1, 2 Peter and Jude

How Should a Christian Live? (1, 2, 3 John)

Higher Ground

Building Your House on the Lord: Marriage and Parenthood

Friendship: Portraits from God's Family Album

Contents

Introduction

I've prayed for the future wives of my sons since they were babies. I've prayed that God would give each of them a woman of value — a woman who will be a wonderful and loving ministry partner — and that God would spare my sons the kind of wife who would ruin them!* (Proverbs 31:3b)

Intriguingly, the Book of Proverbs vividly describes both kinds of women. For example, Proverbs is clear that a woman of value has discretion! (Proverbs 11:22 warns that a beautiful woman who lacks discretion is like a gold ring in a pig's snout!) In each chapter, as we examine a particular quality, we'll look first at the Proverbs which describe this quality, and then at scriptural examples of women who possessed or lacked the particular quality. (See Contents) Having real life examples will etch these characteristics in your heart and mind and help you to become the woman of value God longs for you to be.

It's helpful to know that proverbs are general truths, rather than promises. For example, generally speaking, if you train up a child in the way he should go, he will become a godly adult — but there are exceptions, and they do not disprove the proverb, for proverbs are generalities.

Memory verses are part of each lesson. A sheet with all the verses is at the back of this guide. Cut it out and place it on your mirror or refrigerator!

Leader's helps are also at the back of this guide. *If your group is having trouble finishing on time, the leader's notes will recommend which questions could be skipped in discussion time.*

This guide, by its very nature, tends to focus on behavior. To bring the focus back to Christ, it is suggested that you close your prayer

---

*So far I have one daughter-in-law, and Julie is indeed a woman of value! Pray, mothers, pray!

time with a chorus that honors Christ. A few are printed at the very back of this guide.

If you are naturally shy, star the questions where you feel God has given you something to say. Then take courage and speak up! If you are naturally talkative, do the same thing—and don't star every question. Then hold back on the other questions, so that the shyer people have silent spaces in which to gather the courage to speak up.

Determine now to be faithful in doing your homework. For your convenience, each chapter is divided into five quiet times, for your daily devotions. Also, determine to be faithful in your attendance to your small group. For, as you will see, though faithfulness is rare in our world, a woman of value *is* faithful.

One

She Loves and Fears God
Sapphira/The Hebrew Midwives

W hat causes a woman to be truthful when the truth is humbling? To be faithful when faithfulness is costly? To be a shining light when all around people are being conformed to the darkness? The rarity of people like this is emphasized by the book of Proverbs:

> Many proclaim themselves loyal, but who can find one worthy of trust? (Prov. 20:6, NRSVB)

> A wife of noble character who can find? She is worth far more than rubies (Prov. 31:10).

Yet people like this exist, and like priceless jewels, their value is great, because they are so rare.

Seventeen-year-old Charity Allen was offered a role on "Another World," a successful NBC daytime drama. Stardom, a seven figure salary, and a limousine were dangled in front of her eyes. Her family's days of living in a trailer could be over! Though the producer assured her she wouldn't have to compromise her Christian convictions, the script revealed her character would, among other things, have an affair with a married man. Though the producer argued that these are "adolescent issues that all teens struggle with," Charity responded:

9

How many teens do you know who have affairs with married men? I don't know any! And I'm not going to portray one, either.

Despite pressure from producers, and even from her teachers, Charity stood firm. Her foremost desire was to live a life that was pleasing to God and this didn't fit! "Another World" cast a different girl. Charity gave up being a star. Or did she? Susie Shellenberger, in writing about Charity for *Brio,* (Focus on the Family's May, 1994 magazine for girls) said that Charity, in choosing to live a life that is pleasing to God, shines "like a star amidst a crooked and depraved generation" (Phil. 2:14-15).

Though some might argue with Charity's choice, it's clear that Charity made her decision because she loved and feared God. Charity is a young woman of value.

WARMUP
Read over the introduction together and then have each woman share her name, a little about herself, and what she hopes to gain from the group.

Have each woman share an example (giving women the freedom to pass) of a choice a woman who longs to live a life that is pleasing to God might be asked to make in her home, or place of work, or school, or personal relationships.

Read the following passage:

In the fear of the Lord one has strong confidence, and one's children will have a refuge. The fear of the Lord is a fountain of life, so that one may avoid the snares of death (Prov. 14:26-27).

Describe some "snares" you might be saved from by fearing God. Discuss this in terms of Charity's choice as well.

SCRIPTURE STUDY
The Scripture study is divided into five days, for five personal quiet times with the Lord.

DAY 1

A Woman of Value Fears the Lord

The Book of Proverbs begins and ends with stressing the importance of fearing the Lord.

> The fear of the Lord is the beginning of knowledge, but fools despise wisdom and discipline (Prov. 1:7).

> Charm is deceptive, and beauty is fleeting; but a woman who fears the Lord is to be praised (Prov. 31:30).

Memorize Proverbs 31:30 by taking a word at a time. (Charm; Charm is; Charm is deceptive . . .) A list of memory verses can be found at the end of this guide. Tear them out and hang them on your mirror or above your kitchen sink!

1. What do you learn about the fear of the Lord from the above proverbs?

2. Why do you think the fear of the Lord is the beginning of wisdom? Was that true in your life? If so, explain how.

Throughout the Old and New Testaments, we are exhorted to fear God. This includes the concept of reverence, but also an awakening to the realization of God's holiness and wrath at unrighteousness. This fear helps us understand our need for a Savior. Jesus makes this clear when He says:

> Do not be afraid of those who kill the body but cannot kill the soul. Rather, be afraid of the One who can destroy both soul and body in hell (Matt. 10:28).

In my life, it was the fear of hell that caused me to come to Him and surrender my life to Him. When I placed my trust in Jesus and His payment for my sin on the cross, God delivered me from my fear of hell. Now my love for God is stronger than my fear of Him, but I still fear Him, in the way a child who respects her father fears disobeying and displeasing Him.

11

3. The "fool" in Proverbs is someone who does not fear God. Why is it foolish not to fear God?

If we would know God, it is vital that we face the truth concerning His wrath, however unfashionable it may be, and however strong our initial prejudices against it. Otherwise, we shall not understand the gospel of salvation from wrath, nor the propitiatory achievement of the cross, nor the wonder of the redeeming love of God (J.I. Packer, *Knowing God*, InterVarsity, p. 152).

DAY 2
Fear God, and Fear Nothing Else

A few years after I surrendered my life to Christ, God delivered me from a fear that had plagued me ever since my teens, and that was the fear of being a murder victim of a maniac. When my husband had all-night duty in his medical training, I slept very little and became the bleary-eyed mother of two toddlers. We had a house on the Puget Sound with bedrooms on the lower level facing the water. Any sound in the night terrified me—I'd imagine someone pulling up in a canoe. . . . A sympathetic friend encouraged me to memorize Psalm 34. One sleepless night I paced and memorized. Then I began to pray for protection. Yet doubts assailed me: "But what," I wondered, "if it is God's will for me to die at the hands of a crazed man?" Suddenly, in the still of the night, a voice spoke within me, a voice I knew was God's. He said, "Dee, you *are* going to die —but not that way."

I was amazed. And then curious. I asked the Almighty a question. "What way *am* I going to die?"

Silence. He had told me all I needed to know. In His compassion, He had reached out, comforted His child, and delivered her from her obsessive fear. "As a father has compassion on his children, so the Lord has compassion on those who fear him" (Ps. 103:13).

4. Do you have any fears which plague you? Has God delivered you from any fears? If so, explain.

Read Psalm 34.
5. What promises do you find in verses 7-9? What conditions?

What else stands out to you in this psalm? Why?

DAY 3
Sapphira, A Woman Who Trifled With God

The fear of the Lord adds length to life, but the years of the wicked are cut short (Prov. 10:27).

When I am inclined to embellish the truth to receive praise from others, may I remember Ananias and Sapphira! While there's nothing to indicate that this couple lost their salvation, they certainly lost years on earth and their reputations. Though God usually spares us His wrath, He is still sovereign, and may choose to discipline. It does seem that often believers in leadership who trifle with God are caught and humbled publicly.

Read Acts 4:32-37 as background.
6. Joseph was greatly loved by the body of believers, as evidenced by his nickname. What was it? What act of encouragement is recorded about him in this passage?

Read Acts 5:1-11.
7. Describe the incident in this passage and the effect it had on the church.

In this grace age, we are turning out mediocre saints who feel that since they are in Christ, they can live as they please. But

13

I don't know of anything that will check sin quicker than a deep reverence for God (Charles Swindoll, "Insight for Living," April 7, 1994).

8. How did Peter give Sapphira a second chance to tell the truth? What do you think motivated her to lie?

9. Are you ever motivated to enhance your own significance? If possible, give an example. With whose significance should we be concerned?

Describe some ways that you can see a longing in your heart to bring glory to God.

10. Some Christians insist that if your husband asks you to do something immoral, you should submit because God will hold your husband — not *you* — accountable. How does this passage teach otherwise? Does this mean we should not submit to our husbands? Explain.

DAY 4
The Hebrew Midwives Feared God and Were Blessed
Lori, an unmarried college freshman, discovered she was pregnant. "Because I didn't want to face my parents, I had fleeting thoughts of abortion and even suicide, but my fear of God kept me from either. Today my parents and I cherish my three-year-old daughter and are so thankful God put His fear in me."

Read Exodus 1:8-22.
11. Describe the three plans Pharaoh had for reducing the number of the Israelites.

12. How did the midwives foil plan B? Why did they refuse to cooperate? How did God respond?

During World War II, Corrie ten Boom showed similar courage when she learned that a Jewish orphanage in Amsterdam was to be raided and the babies slaughtered. Dressed in the uniforms of Nazi soldiers who'd defected, thirty teenage boys drove up to the orphanage in trucks and demanded the babies. They took them from the arms of weeping workers who did not realize the babies were actually being saved. Years later Corrie had the privilege of meeting some of these children. In emotional greeting scenes, she hugged them and gave thanks to the Lord (Joan Winmill Brown, *Corrie: The Lives She's Touched,* Revell, p. 31).

DAY 5 . . . .
God Uses the Woman who Fears Him
My sister Sally led me to the Lord when I was a young wife and mother. Because Sally "knows what it is to fear the Lord, she tried to persuade me" to put my trust in Christ (2 Cor. 5:11). The Holy Spirit worked through my sister, and I was persuaded. When I told Sally that my opening chapter was on fearing the Lord and I was a bit apprehensive of a negative reaction, Sally firmly said: "There's no command in the Scripture with more blessings attached to it. Don't fear what others will think, Dee, fear God." Proverbs 29:25 warns: "The fear of man will prove to be a snare." I have come to see that the woman who loves and fears God is used mightily by Him, and the woman who fears others is paralyzed and fails to bear fruit.

13. In your life, think about how the fear of the Lord has led to fruitfulness. Think about receiving Christ, or sharing Christ with others, or making hard choices such as staying at home with your children or taking a low-paying ministry position. Can you share one with the group?

14. What do you think you will remember from this lesson? How will you apply it?

PRAYER TIME

Many people are intimidated by the idea of praying out loud. This guide will be gentle, leading you into this gradually. And no one will ever be forced to pray out loud.

Today, have each woman share a personal request. For example, she might ask, "I would like to grow closer to God" or "I need wisdom as a mother." Write these down, and pray for each other at home. Pay particular attention to the woman on your right, for whom you will pray daily.

Teach your group to sing "Father, I Adore You" (p. 100). (See the hints for leading music on page 100.)

Two

Her Heart Is Fully Devoted to Christ

Martha/Mary

When I was doing my research for *The Lifestyles of Christian Women*, I surveyed 4,000 women who had a personal relationship with Christ. I wanted to know: "Does knowing Christ make a difference in the way we live?" I was encouraged to find that it did, though for some women the difference was minimal. *Other women were living lives that were so transformed that I found myself convicted and challenged by their whole-hearted devotion.*

Whenever I found a survey from a woman like that, I put it in what I began to label as my "Remnant File." When I finished going through the forms, I went back through my "Remnant File" to see if *those* women had anything in common. Remarkably, one discipline was found in *every* form. The women in my "Remnant File" made it a priority to spend time with the Lord each day in Bible study and prayer. (Intriguingly, there was a correlating habit that was almost as consistent: these women spent very little time watching TV. Perhaps not having that distraction freed them to have time to fill their heart with the things of the Lord through Bible study, Christian radio, and Christian books.) One thing that I could not measure in my survey forms was their heart — and yet one clear evidence of a heart that is truly devoted to Christ is the desire to spend time with Him, to talk to Him, and, like Mary of Bethany, to sit at His feet.

17

WARMUP

Mary of Bethany is remembered for her single-hearted devotion to Jesus. In that devotion, she experienced joy. Joy can come through being aware of His love for you, being led by His Word, or a myriad of other ways. Go around the room, giving women the freedom to pass, and ask them to finish the sentence: **One time when I experienced joy in Jesus recently was . . .**

DAY 1
. . . .
She Keeps Her Heart With All Diligence

The heart is key to all of life. Seventy-five times in the book of Proverbs alone (KJV) the word *heart* is used. The root reason for a ho-hum Christian life is a divided and distracted heart: a failure to keep our hearts with all diligence. Memorize the following:

> Keep thy heart with all diligence, for out of it are the issues of life (Prov. 4:23, KJV).

1. Put the above proverb in your own words.

2. The following passages in proverbs give insight on how to keep our hearts with all diligence. Write down any principles you find in the passages for keeping your heart.

    A. Proverbs 2:1-6

    B. Proverbs 3:3-8

Heart Examination!
For Personal Reflection Only

3. Consider the following ways to keep your heart healthy. How could you improve in each?

    A. Your daily time of Bible study and prayer

    B. Memorizing Scripture

18

C. Keeping the path clear between you and the Lord through confessing and turning from any sin

D. Listening to Christian music or radio; reading Christian books or magazines:

Action Assignment. Plan when and where you will have your daily time of Bible study and prayer this week. Keep this appointment as diligently as you would keep appointments with people.

When will you meet with God?

Where will you meet with Him?

DAY 2
. . . .
She Understands the Importance of a Pure Heart
Review your memory work of Proverbs 4:23.

4. In order to have a pure heart, an individual must first put her trust in Christ. What is the central thought in each of the following passages?

   A. Who can say, "I have kept my heart pure; I am clean and without sin"? (Prov. 20:9)

   B. Now God says He will accept and acquit us—declare us "not guilty"—if we trust Jesus Christ to take away our sins. And we all can be saved in this same way, by coming to Christ, no matter who we are or what we have been like. Yes, all have sinned; all fall short of God's glorious ideal; yet now God declares us "not guilty" of offending Him if we trust in Jesus Christ, who in His kindness freely takes away our sins. For God sent Christ Jesus to take the punishment for our sins and to end all God's anger against us (Rom. 3:22b-25a, TLB).

C. That if you confess with your mouth, "Jesus is Lord," and believe in your heart that God raised Him from the dead, you will be saved (Rom. 10:9).

Although there is only one way to God—through Christ—individuals come in many ways to Christ. Some have faith in Christ's way of salvation when they are little children, as Timothy did. They may not remember when they trusted Christ, but they are certain that He is their Savior. Others have a dramatic conversion as adults, like Paul on the road to Damascus. Others would describe themselves as Timothy-Pauls, having responded as children, drifted away, but returned to their faith in later years.

5. Would you describe yourself as a Timothy, a Paul, a Timothy-Paul, or as someone who is still on the way? (Ask several volunteers to share their stories *in a sentence or two.*)

DAY 3
She Has a Teachable Heart
It is possible to be a church-goer, to be involved in ministry, and even to be spending time reading the Bible, and yet have a heart that is far from the Lord.

In the Book of Isaiah, God's people had a heart problem. Read the following passage and describe the problem.

The Lord says: "These people come near to me with their mouth and honor me with their lips, but their hearts are far from me. Their worship of me is made up only of rules taught my men" (Isa. 29:13).

6. How can you guard against being like the people described in Isaiah?

7. Turn to Psalm 32. What insight can you glean from the following verses about keeping your heart tender and pure?

    A. Psalm 32:1-5

    B. Psalm 32:6-7

    C. Psalm 32:8-9

    D. Psalm 32:11

Spiritual awakening always begins with cleansing. It begins in the heart of an individual who suddenly says to himself, "I'm dirty." And that is painful, particularly if we've been pretending all along to be clean. We go kicking and protesting to the water basin — we'll give our faces a swipe, but we don't want to wash behind our ears. . . . but pure joy can be experienced in the bathtub . . . God delights in the spiritual bathing of his earthly children and he wraps them, cleansed, in the wooly towel of his love and approval (Karen Mains, *With My Whole Heart*, Multnomah, p. 19).

8. God may rebuke us through His Word, His Spirit, or through one of His servants. Read the following and explain why we should listen carefully to rebuke.

    A. Proverbs 1:22-33

    B. Proverbs 15:31-32

9. Share a time when you listened to rebuke from God or a friend and were glad you did.

Dawson Trotman, who founded the International Discipleship Ministry of Navigators, said that whenever he is criticized, he always takes it into his prayer closet with the Lord and asks God to show him if there is a kernel of truth in the criticism (Dawson Trotman, *Daws*, NavPress).

DAY 4
. . . .
A Devoted Heart: Mary of Bethany
A Distracted Heart: Martha of Bethany
Review your memory work of Proverbs 4:23.

We are told that Jesus loved both Mary and Martha of Bethany (John 11:5), and many times the one who had "no place to lay his head" found rest and refreshment in their hospitable home. The scene we remember the best, however, is when Jesus gently rebuked Martha. Though most of us as women can empathize with Martha, be sure you don't miss appreciating Mary, or you'll miss the main point!

Read Luke 10:38-42
10. As this tends to be a familiar passage, look at it carefully. Write down any phrases which describe Mary. Write down any phrases which describe Martha.

    Mary:

    Martha:

Jeanne Hendricks tells of one Thanksgiving when she particularly empathized with Martha.

> The Lord and I had many conversations about the fact that the house was too small, but He kept saying "wait" . . . Shortly before it was time to serve the meal, I slipped into the hot kitchen to check on my roasting turkey. As I was lifting it from one place to another in a space too tight for efficient operation, it slipped and fell right down on the floor! Suddenly I felt a surge of self-pity. I leaned up against the wall and tears of frustration came to my eyes. In my heart

22

I said, "Lord, I told You so! Now look what's happened! It's all Your fault!" Then I heard laughter and talking from the other room and I suddenly felt ashamed. What if somebody should come and see me crumpled in such dejection? ... Jesus did not scold Martha for what she was doing. Martha had a servant heart and the Lord honored that attitude; it was her superficial robe of self-pity which caught his scorn (Jeanne Hendricks, *A Woman For All Seasons*, Thomas Nelson, pp. 155-56).

For Personal Reflection Only

11. In what ways do you tend to feel sorry for yourself? What do you think Jesus would say to you?

Because Jesus wanted the best for Martha he was saying: "Things of temporal value, worries about this life, choke My Word and darken your view of eternal matters" (Gien Garssen, *Her Name is Woman,* NavPress, p. 162).

12. What advice would you give the woman who is too distracted with her life to spend time daily in God's Word?

Early in my Christian life I realized that if I don't have time for the Lord in prayer and Bible study, I really cannot say He is first in my life. That voice that tells me "to just put a load of wash in (or whatever!) before I spend time with God" may very well be the voice of the evil one, who longs to distract me from what is most important.

DAY 5
Martha of Bethany, a Teachable Heart
Mary of Bethany, an Enlightened Heart
If you are not familiar with the story of Jesus raising Lazarus, the brother of Martha and Mary, read it (John 11:1-43).

13. Read John 12:1-2.

A. How is Martha's character similar to the account of her in Luke?

B. How is it also different? Why do you think this is?

C. If you have a gift of serving, or of hospitality, as Martha did, how can you learn, as Martha did, to not be so task-oriented that you lose sight of what is best?

14. Read John 12:3-11

A. Describe Mary of Bethany's courageous act.

B. What does Jesus tell Judas when Judas objects?

Matthew 26:12-13 records a fuller response from Jesus: "When she poured this perfume on my body, she did it to prepare me for burial. I tell you the truth, wherever this Gospel is preached throughout the world, what she has done will also be told, in memory of her." God rewarded Mary's whole-hearted devotion with a rare enlightenment. In his study Bible, C.I. Scofield comments: "Mary of Bethany, alone of our Lord's followers, comprehended His thrice-repeated announcement of His coming death and resurrection." God enlightens those who hunger and thirst for Him.

15. What do you want to remember from the example of Mary of Bethany?

PRAYER TIME

An unintimidating form of group prayer is "Conversational Prayer," also called "Popcorn Prayer." The leader introduces a subject, or the name of a group member, and then as many women as wish offer a simple sentence. Then, when the "popping" stops, the leader lifts up the name of another group member. Take prayer requests. Then pray, using Popcorn Prayer. Close by singing "Father, I Adore You" (p. 100). This song can also be sung in a round.

POPCORN PRAYER

1. **Introduce one person or subject at a time.**
2. **Prayers should be short "pops" from anyone anywhere in the circle.**
3. **Continue until "popping" stops.**
4. **Introduce another person or subject.**

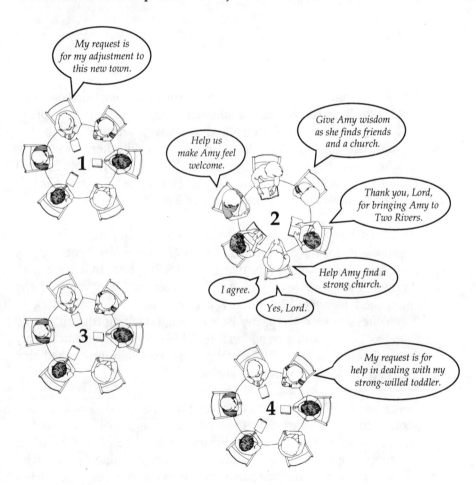

25

Three

She Speaks with Wisdom
Penninah/Hannah

Yesterday I became very angry with Beth, our thirteen-year-old daughter whom we adopted a year ago from an orphanage in Bangkok. Ostensibly I was angry because Beth hadn't finished the laundry. After losing my temper with her, I went into another room to cool down. Sensing a check from the Holy Spirit, I defended myself. *But, Lord, it was right for me to scold her. She told me she'd finished the laundry and she hadn't.*

The Lord revealed to me that while speaking the truth in love was appropriate, losing my temper was not. The real reason for my disproportionate anger was that I was feeling hurt that Beth isn't warmer and more loving to me. The root problem was not the unfinished laundry, and not even disobedience, but my lack of forgiveness toward Beth, my lack of understanding toward a child who has built a wall around herself. I'd been storing up hurt in my heart, keeping a record of slights, and eventually unleashed that hurt over a load of unfolded socks.

Jesus says: "The good man brings good things out of the good stored up in his heart, and the evil man brings evil things out of the evil stored up in his heart. For out of the overflow of his heart his mouth speaks" (Luke 6:45). A woman of value speaks with kindness and wisdom, because that is what is stored up in her heart.

WARMUP

Go around, giving women the freedom to pass, and ask: **Think about a significant conversation that you had with someone recently that was to you "a fountain of life" (Prov. 10:11). What about it made it refreshing?**

On-the-Spot Action Assignment. In every discussion group, there are usually women who are too quick to speak up and others who are too slow. This exercise is to help you discern whether you lean toward either being a monopolizer or a wallflower. Your leader will give each woman five pennies. Every time you speak, put a penny in your lap. After you've spent your pennies, let the others speak. And everyone should spend their pennies!

SCRIPTURE STUDY
DAY 1
. . . .
She Understands How Her Heart Affects Her Speech
Review your first two memory passages:

> Charm is deceptive, and beauty is fleeting; but a woman who fears the Lord is to be praised (Prov. 31:30).

> Keep thy heart with all diligence, for out of it are the issues of life (Prov. 4:23, KJV).

Now add the following:

> She speaks with wisdom, and faithful instruction is on her tongue (Prov. 31:26).

1. Explain how the above passages are related.

When I am depleted spiritually, I become angry more quickly and either start a quarrel or enter one at the first provocation. When my walk with God is vital, somehow He keeps my emotional well-being stable. A time of drinking deeply from the river of His delights brings me joy and peace (Carole Mayhall, *Words That Hurt, Words That Heal*, NavPress, pp. 65-66).

2. In each of the following, explain the heart's effect on the tongue.

Out of the same mouth come praise and cursing. My brothers, this should not be. Can both fresh water and salt water flow from the same spring? My brothers, can a fig tree bear olives, or a grapevine bear figs? Neither can a salt spring produce fresh water (James 3:10-12).

The heart of the righteous weighs its answers but the mouth of the wicked gushes evil (Prov. 15:28).

A wise man's heart guides his mouth, and his lips promote instruction (Prov. 16:23).

3. What ideas do you have for guiding mealtime conversations with friends or family so that they become a "fountain of life"?

We have a family policy not to use mealtimes to discuss problems, discipline, or schedules, but instead to reserve that time for bonding and encouragement. Often I ask a question (**What was the most interesting moment of your day?**), or we discuss an ethical dilemma (*Ungame* or *Scruples* game cards are great for this!), or we each share what we've learned from our quiet times and interact about it.

4. Jesus says that out of the overflow of the heart the mouth speaks (Matt. 12:34b). If the heart is full of football, that's going to be the topic of conversation! What are your most frequent topics of conversation?

If the above list deals primarily with transitory things, what life changes could you make so that the overflow of your heart would spill forth eternally encouraging things?

Action Assignment. "The mouth of the righteous is a fountain of life" (Prov. 10:11). Choose to do one of the following this week.

    A. Read a Christian book this week and journal one new thought to share with the group.
    B. Listen to Christian radio and journal one new thought to share with the group. (If you're not keeping a journal, start! Record what you learn from God's Word, sermons, books, etc. This exercise alone will change your heart and its overflow!)

DAY 2
She Refrains From Boasting and Quarreling
Boasting!

5. Boasting springs from a prideful heart. Record the main point of the following proverbs in your own words.

    Let another praise you, and not your own mouth; someone else, and not your own lips (Prov. 27:2).

    It is not good to eat too much honey, nor is it honorable to seek one's own honor (Prov. 25:27).

    If you want people to think well of you, do not speak well of yourself (Pascal).

Quarreling!

    But the wisdom that comes from heaven is first of all pure, then peace-loving, considerate, submissive, full of mercy and good fruit, impartial and sincere. Peacemakers who sow in peace raise a harvest of righteousness. What causes fights and quarrels among you? Don't they come from your desires that battle within you? You want something but don't get it. You kill and covet, but you cannot have what you want. You quarrel and fight (James 3:17–4:2a).

    Only by pride cometh contention: but with the well advised is wisdom (Prov. 13:10, KJV).

6. What is the source of quarrels, according to the above?

   How can you discern between a healthy difference of opinion and a quarrel?

7. Anger is not necessarily sinful, for Jesus became angry. However, how we handle anger *can* be sinful. Read the following passages and summarize what you learn about dealing with or expressing anger.

   And the Lord's servant must not quarrel, instead, he must be kind to everyone, able to teach, not resentful (2 Tim. 2:24).

   It is honorable to refrain from strife, but every fool is quick to quarrel (Prov. 20:3, NRSVB).

   Do not let the sun go down while you are still angry and do not give the devil a foothold (Eph. 4:26-27).

   What divides and severs true Christian groups and Christians — what leaves a bitterness that can last for 20, 30, or 40 years is not the issue of doctrine or belief which caused the differences in the first place. Invariably it is lack of love — and the bitter things that are said by true Christians in the midst of differences. These stick in the mind like glue. . . . It is these things — these unloving attitudes and words — that cause the stench that the world can smell . . . But Jesus did give the mark that will arrest the attention of the world . . . What is it? The love that true Christians show for each other and not just for their own party (Francis Schaeffer, "The Mark of a Christian" in *The Church at the End of the 20th Century,* InterVarsity, p. 144).

DAY 3
She Is Quick to Listen, Slow to Speak, and Slow to Become Angry

With company coming for dinner, Carole grimly tackled the dirty job of cleaning the barbecue grill. Her husband, Jack, was resting with his feet up on the ottoman, having just come in from his new exercise program. When Carole came in for more paper towels, he told her, proudly, "I walked five miles today.

Without a thought, Carole said: "Boy, just think of all you could have accomplished with that kind of energy." Seeing the joy of accomplishment drain from her husband's face, Carole felt convicted. She said, "I wanted to reach out and pull the words back. . . . I apologized profusely and Jack said he forgave me. But the words had been said. I could not undo that. I remembered the verse that says, 'He who guards his lips guards his soul, but he who speaks rashly will come to ruin' (Prov. 13:3)" (Carole Mayhall, *Words that Hurt, Words that Heal*, NavPress, pp. 45-46).

8. Read the following proverbs and then describe the various kinds of damage a reckless woman might cause or a thoughtful woman might avoid.

   An evil man is trapped by his sinful talk, but a righteous man escapes trouble (Prov. 12:13).

   Reckless words pierce like a sword (Prov. 12:18).

   A harsh word stirs up anger (Prov. 15:1b).

   When words are many, sin is not absent, but he who holds his tongue is wise (Prov. 10:19).

9. Give an example of trouble you caused or avoided by how you used or controlled your tongue.

DAY 4
She Consciously Uses Her Tongue For Good
How thankful I am for godly friends who affirm me, who draw out the deep waters of my soul with questions, and who sharpen me

with discussions out of the overflow of their own rich hearts! They understand the "tongue has the power of life and death" (Prov. 18:21) and use it to bring life.

10. Read the following passages carefully. Then list some ways the tongue can be used for good.

    An anxious heart weighs a man down, but a kind word cheers him up (Prov. 12:25).

    Pleasant words are a honeycomb, sweet to the soul and healing to the bones (Prov. 16:24).

    Perfume and incense bring joy to the heart, and the pleasantness of one's friends springs from his earnest counsel (Prov. 27:9).

On-the-Spot Action Assignment. If time permits, go around the room and have each woman say one affirming sentence about the woman on her right. (You could divide into groups of three or four to do this more quickly.)

11. Thoughtful, affirming, pleasant, and wise words bless others, but they also impact the giver. Explain the following verse.

    From the fruit of his lips a man is filled with good things as surely as the work of his hands rewards him (Prov. 12:14).

    How have you been rewarded by using your tongue for good?

12. Have you ever had the experience of not understanding your own heart, or hurt, or reasons for doing something—but a friend was able to draw you out and help you to understand yourself? If you can remember a specific instance, share.

How could you better put Proverbs 12:14 into practice with others?

In your personal quiet time, use your tongue for good by singing praises to God, using the songs in the back of this guide.

DAY 5
. . . .
Penninah and Hannah
Penninah and Hannah were both married to the same man. In addition to the pain of this relationship, each woman had her own private pain. Penninah responded to that pain foolishly, and Hannah responded wisely.

Read 1 Samuel 1:1-11. (In discussion, read only verses 6-11.)
13. Describe Penninah's private pain. How did she respond to it?

What kind of feelings tempt someone to behave as Penninah did?

14. Describe Hannah's private pain. How did she respond to it?

When our cup is jostled, what spills out reveals what is inside. How would you describe Hannah's heart, and how do you think it got that way?

Read 1 Samuel 1:12-28. (In discussion, read verses 12-16.)
15. How did Hannah respond to Eli?

How did God bless Hannah? Do you think the story might have turned out differently had Hannah become angry with Eli?

Hannah kept her vow to God and relinquished Samuel. How do you think she was able to do it?

16. Read Hannah's song in 1 Samuel 2:1-10 and list everything you can discover which Hannah knew about God.

Hannah's song of praise may very well have been the inspiration for Mary's Magnificat. Hannah and Mary both regarded themselves as "handmaidens" of the Lord and were eager to serve their great God. Most of us pray in hard times, but a truly godly woman also prays in good times.

17. Does this song give you any insight as to why Hannah was able to be quiet when Peninnah taunted her?

What helps you control your tongue when someone is unkind to you?

18. Which response to pain was more effective? Peninnah's or Hannah's? Why?

19. What do you learn from this story to apply to your own life?

For Personal Reflection Only
How many of your pennies did you spend? Do you talk too much, too easily, or too long? Do you talk too little and deprive the group of rich interaction? How could you do better?

One of the most difficult problems for any Bible study discussion facilitator is the monopolizer. If you know you have a tendency toward monopolizing, ask a friend to sit next to you and give you a gentle pat when you need it. A group is also impoverished if the shy people never share. Mark the questions where you feel you might have something to offer, and then speak up!

PRAYER TIME
Spend some time using your tongues in praise to God, encouraging the women to say simple sentences of thanks or praise. Then close by singing the "Doxology" (p. 101).

Four

She Is Discreet

The Haughty Women of Zion/The Holy Women of Old

H ow do you describe femininity? The essence of woman-
hood is difficult to define, but it's as recognizable as the
fragrance of lilacs. One woman who had this quality and
captured the respect of the world was Jacqueline Kennedy Onas-
sis. When she died, the following tributes were typical:

> She was a connection to a time that was more dignified, more
> private, an America in which standards were higher and
> clearer and elegance meant something . . . She had manners,
> the kind that remind us that manners spring from a certain
> moral view—that you do tribute to the world and the people
> in it by being kind and showing respect, by sending the note
> and the flowers, by being loyal, and cheering a friend (Peggy
> Noonan, *Time Magazine*, 5/30/94).
>
> I am struck most by how we reflect on her taste and passion
> for the highest of excellence, while we live in a base society.
> We mourn the loss of her desire for privacy in an expose-all
> world and miss her innocence in a country filled with people
> eager to experience everything. We mourn the loss of Jac-
> queline Bouvier Kennedy Onassis' grace in this graceless
> society (Stu Koblentz, *Time Magazine*, 6/20/94).

Webster defines *discretion* as the quality of being discerning or
discriminating. Likewise, one of the Hebrew definitions of the

word that is translated *discretion* is "taste." A lady knows what is in good taste. My mother always taught us that a lady doesn't wear too much make-up, show too much of her body, use vulgar language, or chew gum in public. However, discretion goes deeper than this. For it is possible for a woman to win favor with the world because she has grace and elegance, and yet not win favor with God. Another definition of discretion in Webster's Dictionary is: "the act of separating, the state or quality of being separate or distinct." As Christians, we are told to remember that we are "a chosen people, a royal priesthood, a holy nation, a people belonging to God" (1 Peter 2:9). And women are exhorted to behave "as is appropriate for women who profess to worship God" (1 Tim. 2:10). This kind of behavior begins in the heart, with a surrender to God, and is developed through abiding in Christ and His Word.

WARMUP
Go around your circle, giving women the freedom to pass, and have each woman share an example of ladylikeness or unladylikeness, of poise or the lack of it. (Don't worry about repetition — God may use it to drum home a point!)

If new women have joined your group, introduce them and have them tell a little about themselves.

SCRIPTURE STUDY
DAY 1 . . . .
The Loveliness of Discretion
Review the introduction.
1. Solomon described his bride as being "like a lily among thorns" (Song of Songs 2:2). Can you think of a contemporary woman who exemplifies this kind of striking loveliness — who is beautiful because she has poise and integrity? (Try to choose someone the others in the group would know.) Who is she and why do you admire her?

Memorize the following proverb.

Like a gold ring in a pig's snout is a beautiful woman who shows no discretion (Prov. 11:22).

2. What do you think this proverb means? Can you give some examples of how a lovely woman's image can be ruined by her words or behavior?

DAY 2
. . . .
A Woman of Discretion Embraces
Her Identity as a Woman

In *Let Me Be A Woman* (Tyndale), Elisabeth Elliot tells how she and her husband prayed for a son, but were given a daughter. Elisabeth could see her husband's face when the doctor said, "It's a girl." Jim smiled at his wife and said at once, "Her name is Valerie." When Valerie became a young woman, her mother wrote to her:

> We sometimes hear the expression "the accident of sex," as though one's being a man or a woman were a triviality. It is our nature. It is the modality under which we live all our lives; it is what you and I are called to be—called by God, this God who is in charge. It is our destiny, planned, ordained, fulfilled by an all-wise, all-powerful, all-loving Lord.

The central theme of 1 Peter is that we are called for a purpose, and that purpose is to glorify God. Peter urges us to understand our identity as Christians, that we are set apart to be holy. He also has special additional insights from God for women. And though these insights are in the context of marriage, the qualities are applicable to single women as well. All women are to behave with purity and reverence, and though single women do not have a husband to whom they should submit, still, all believers are exhorted to live in submission to one another.

Read 1 Peter 3:1-6.

3. What specific instructions does Peter give to women who are married to unbelievers?

4. Contemplate each of the following phrases, looking at them in additional translations for more insight. For each word or

phrase, give an example of a behavior which would demonstrate this quality.

Purity

Reverence

Unfading beauty of a gentle and quiet spirit

In your personal quiet time sing "For the Beauty of the Earth" (p. 102). Gentleness and contentment springs from a worshipful and thankful heart.

5. Describe how God feels about a woman who has the above characteristics (v. 4).

6. How did Sarah show respect for Abraham? If you are married, how do you show respect for your husband?

DAY 3
A Woman of Discretion Avoids Excesses
Temperance, or moderation, is the characteristic that recognizes that God's good gifts can be abused and ruined. It is intriguing to me that it has often been women who have carried the baton of temperance in our society. As guardians of the home, perhaps women have been the first to see the threat of intemperance to the family. For example, women fought against the legalization of alcohol with "The Women's Christian Temperance Union." Sister organizations of a more contemporary flavor have sprung up to fight the abuse of sex as seen in pornography, TV, and rock music. Food, sex, conversation, and material blessings are all good gifts but must be tempered with wisdom. A woman of discretion guards against excesses in her life and allows her life to shine as a light to a society which is destroying itself through intemperance.

7. In each of the following Proverbs, the phrase "too much" indicates an area where we should exercise moderation. Define the area where we are to guard against excess and then put the proverb in your own words.

A gossip destroys a confidence, so avoid a man who talks too much (Prov. 20:19).

Do not join those who drink too much wine or gorge themselves on meat (Prov. 23:20).

Seldom set foot in your neighbor's house - too much of you and he will hate you (Prov. 25:17).

It is not good to eat too much honey, nor is it honorable to seek one's own honor (Prov. 25:27).

Two things I ask of you, O Lord . . . give me neither poverty nor riches, but give me only my daily bread. Otherwise I may have too much and disown you and say, "Who is the Lord?" Or I may become poor and steal, and so dishonor the name of my God (Prov. 30:7-9).

8. Which of the above proverbs speaks most loudly to you? Why?

Read Isaiah 3:16-24.
9. Describe the women of Zion. How many items of finery did they have?

Do you think that women today spend too much energy, thought, and money on their physical appearance? How would you assess your priorities regarding your own physical appearance?

Anne Ortlund explains why her study of the Proverbs 31 woman led her to make a pact with the Lord to limit the time she spends on her appearance to no more than an hour a day.

> I noticed that twenty-two verses describe this woman's kindness, godliness, hard work, loving relationships — and only one verse out of the twenty-two describes how she looked. . . . Seeing this kind of proportion . . . I prayed, "Father, I want to give 1/22 of my time to making myself as outwardly beautiful as I can; and I want to give all the rest of my time, 21/22 of my life, to becoming wise, kind, godly, hard-working, and the rest" (Anne Ortlund, *The Disciplines of the Beautiful Woman,* Word, p. 45).

10. In what areas is God asking your to exercise moderation?

There are two areas where God tells us *not* to exercise moderation, and that is in loving Him and loving our neighbor. When Jesus was asked what the greatest commandment was, He answered:

> Love the Lord your God with all your heart and with all your soul and with all your mind. . . . And love your neighbor as yourself (Matt. 22:37-39).

Mother Theresa is a woman who exemplifies abstinence or moderation in areas of food, sex, alcohol, and material things. But she is completely immoderate in loving God and loving her neighbor. And she is a woman of value.

DAY 4
The Woman Wisdom
Throughout the Book of Proverbs, there are two voices calling out to all of us. Both of these voices are personified as women: one is the Woman Wisdom, and the other is the Woman Folly. Today we'll consider the Woman Wisdom. She is personified as a hostess who is inviting all who will come to a sumptuous banquet of God's wisdom. There is rich provision for the choices we make for our lives in God's Word, if only we will feed upon it and digest it. A

41

woman of discretion listens carefully to the voice of Wisdom, the voice of God's Word.

Read Proverbs 9:1-6.
11. What are some of the phrases which tell us of the strength and richness of God's wisdom?

    Which phrases show us that this wisdom is offered to all?

The Woman Wisdom entreats us to "leave our simple ways and walk in the way of understanding." *Simple,* in the Hebrew, means "foolish, or easily seduced." We can all be easily seduced by the world without God's Wisdom. Share one way that God has opened your eyes with His Word and helped you to leave a "simple or foolish path" and taken instead the higher and wiser road.

Read Proverbs 1:20-23.
12. In the above passage, what other reason does the Woman Wisdom give for responding to God's Word? (v. 23) Have you found this to be true?

    How do you discipline yourself to spend time in God's Word? What could you do to strengthen this habit or to make your time more meaningful?

DAY 5 ....
The Woman Folly
Review your memory verse of Proverbs 11:22.

Read Proverbs 9:13-18.
13. What phrases are used to describe the Woman Folly?

    What lie does the Woman Folly tell to those who pass by? What makes this lie believable?

14. What warning do you find for your life in this passage?

15. In summary, describe a woman of discretion. What lesson has God particularly impressed on your heart?

PRAYER TIME

One effective way to pray in God's will is to pray through Scripture. Pair off in twos and pray through 1 Peter 3:2-4 for one another. For example, if I were paired with Lisa, a young single, I might pray:

Father, I pray for reverence for you to grow in Lisa's heart. Help her to draw near to you and keep your holiness in mind. Keep her thoughts and actions pure. Help her to trust you with her fears—of her upcoming exam, of her desire to be married, of her dwindling finances. Fill her with the quiet beauty that comes from trusting you.

Five

She Is Prudent
Zeresh/Abigail

When Lemuel's mother gave him guidelines on what to look for in a woman of value, prudence was near the top of her list. A pretty playmate could ruin him! In her book, *The Complete Woman,* Patricia Gundry explains that while it may seem unromantic to look for a wife who knows how to handle responsibility and money wisely, many men would be much less stressed had they allowed their heads as well as their hearts to help them choose life partners. A wise man watches to see how a woman handles her finances, her housekeeping, and her temper. And he *prays* for a godly, loving, and prudent wife, for God says:

> Houses and wealth are inherited from parents, but a prudent wife is from the Lord (Prov. 19:14).

One possible meaning in the above proverb is that an imprudent wife may squander away any wealth that a man has inherited, but a prudent wife helps him to handle his money wisely. I interviewed one such wife recently, who is also the mother of seven sons. Cindy Sutphin told me the following story:

> Seven years ago we were $10,000 in debt and not tithing. Under conviction, I prayed for wisdom and the Lord gave me a plan: if we moved to a less expensive home in the country, we could obey the Lord in the area of finances. When I suggested this to my husband Mark, he agreed—because the

Lord had been dealing with him too! Not only were we able to pay off our debt and practice tithing, but we were richly blessed by our life in the country. During this time Mark realized that our love of the outdoors made us and our seven sons a perfect fit for a camping ministry. Today Mark is at Grace College of the Bible preparing for just such a ministry!

Whether we are single or married, prudence is a characteristic which God values and which we should seek to cultivate. Prudence has to do with making wise choices: with money, with time, and with people.

WARMUP
Reread the previous paragraph. Then go around the circle, asking women to finish the following sentence: **Last week I showed prudence (or imprudence) when I . . .**

Ask for volunteers to recite the proverbs you've memorized so far.

SCRIPTURE STUDY
DAY 1
The Prudent Woman Considers Her Steps
Memorize the following:

> Houses and wealth are inherited from parents, but a prudent wife is from the Lord (Prov. 19:14).

Proverbs 14:8a says: "The wisdom of the prudent is to give thought to their ways." Susannah Wesley echoed this thought when she warned:

> Do not live like the rest of mankind, who pass through the world like straws upon a river, which are carried which way the stream or wind drives them.

1. Make a list of the three most important things you wish to accomplish with your life. What are you doing to accomplish these goals? How could you be more prudent?

Action Assignment. What are the most important things you wish to accomplish today? Prioritize and plan your schedule so that the most important things will be accomplished.

DAY 2
. . . .
The Prudent Woman Plans Ahead
2. How did yesterday's Action Assignment affect your day?

Life simply happens to the imprudent. They don't think ahead to eternity, let alone to the next month. They purchase things impulsively, say whatever comes into their head, and lack caution in explosive situations. The prudent behave very differently.

3. Explain how the prudent behave in each of the following passages. Record also any personal applications.

A prudent man is reluctant to display his knowledge, but the heart of (self-confident) fools proclaims their folly (Prov. 12:23, AMP).

The prudent see danger and take refuge, but the simple keep going and suffer for it (Prov. 27:12).

She sees that her trading is profitable, and her lamp does not go out at night (Prov. 31:18).

"Her lamp does not go out at night" simply means that she has remembered to buy sufficient oil for her lamp. The imprudent can identify with Erma Bombeck who tells her neighbors that if they need anything at the grocery store to let her know, because she goes every two hours!

46

4. How have you planned ahead for:

The grocery store?

An emergency in your car?

Your own spiritual growth?

Eternity?

DAY 3
She Handles Volatile Situations Prudently

When my friend Lee came to Christ, her old friends were critical of her new faith. At a coffee, I listened as they told her that she'd "become a fanatic" and was "taking the Bible too literally." Lee listened quietly, respectfully.

"All I know," Lee said sincerely, "is that Jesus has changed my life." After the coffee, she kept loving those friends and finding ways to minister to their needs. In time, a few came to her Bible study and two came to know Christ. A prudent woman doesn't lose her cool! Thoughtfully, prayerfully, she determines how God would have her resolve conflict, and then she acts, trusting God to be with her.

5. What wisdom do each of the following proverbs give you in dealing with people?

12:16:

15:1:

15:5:

16:7:

6. Is God speaking to you through any of the above? If so, how?

DAY 4
. . . .
Zeresh, An Imprudent Woman
Read Esther 5:9-14.

7. How did Zeresh, Haman's wife, respond when he came home petulant about Mordecai's refusal to bow down to him?

Read Esther 7.

8. How did Zeresh's response to Haman backfire?

Can you think of a time when your lack of prudence caused suffering for you or those close to you? If so, what is God teaching you?

Keeping cool is important in volatile situations. However, a prudent woman needs to do more than refrain from losing her temper. She needs a plan that is inspired by the Spirit of God. Esther exemplified this — she spent three days fasting before she approached her volatile husband. God gave her incredible wisdom, timing, and power.

9. If you have drawn upon God's wisdom in a time of fasting and prayer before moving ahead in an important area, share something about it.

DAY 5
. . . .
Abigail, an Example of Prudence
Author Brenda Wilbee, in *Taming the Dragons,* gives insight on how women have creatively resolved conflict in their lives. She says that often Christian women are discouraged from taking action, but instead told to wait for rescue. However, Scripture gives examples of women like Deborah, Hannah, and Abigail, who asked God for a plan, took action, and experienced victory.

Read 1 Samuel 25:1-17.

10. In the above passage, how is Abigail described? How is her husband Nabal described?

11. How had David and his men been helpful to Nabal and his men in the past? Note everything you can about their behavior.

    How did Nabal respond to the request? Note everything you can about his behavior.

12. Describe the conflict Abigail faced as described to her by the servant.

Read 1 Samuel 25:18-35.
Brenda Wilbee describes Abigail's method as "naming and taming conflict."

"My Lord, pay no attention to that wicked man Nabal," she said, cutting to the quick of the conflict by naming the truth. "He is just like his name—his name is Fool, and folly goes with him."

What? Call your husband a fool? . . . What wife has the right to malign her husband, for whatever reason?

But Abigail was not maligning anyone. "Please," she said to David, still bowed before him. "Forgive Nabal's offense."

A wizard, she was not out to create trouble, but to resolve it. . . . shrewd yet innocent, Abigail saw and named the deepest level of the dilemma, her husband's folly—and then went on to seek creative alternatives, and the dragon was transformed (Brenda Wilbee, *Taming the Dragons*, Harper-Collins).

13. Find ways that Abigail creatively "tamed the dragon" of David's anger. What principles do you see which could be helpful to you?

14. Are you experiencing a challenge in your life? Can you learn anything from Abigail that might help? If so, what?

Read 1 Samuel 25:36-42.
15. Describe what happened to Nabal, Abigail, and David.

16. How does Abigail exemplify prudence?

PRAYER TIME
Pray conversationally for one another's challenges (Question #14), using Popcorn Prayer. Ask God for a plan! Close by singing "Turn Your Eyes Upon Jesus" (p. 103)

Six

She Honors Her Husband
Rebekah/Elizabeth

My husband and I came to Christ early in our marriage, but as a baby Christian, I failed to truly honor my husband. His hours in medical training were long, and I nagged him about it like the woman in Proverbs who is compared to the "drip, drip, drip" of a faucet! But through the Scriptures, a growing reverence for the Lord, and godly women who mentored me, my attitude and behavior toward Steve changed. As I sought to show my husband honor, wonderful things occurred in our marriage. He was so grateful for the change in my behavior, that he did all he could to honor me. Today we have been married thirty years and have five children and a grandchild. We spend time each day in intimate conversation, we cannot remember the last time a cross word passed between us, and our hearts fill with joyful anticipation when we are reunited after our day's activities each evening.

WARMUP
Go around the circle, asking women to share one example of a way a woman might show her husband honor, or fail to show him honor. Pair off and review your memory verses.

SCRIPTURE STUDY
DAY 1
She Brings Him Good All The Days of Her Life
Memorize the following passage.

A wife of noble character who can find? She is worth far more than rubies. Her husband has full confidence in her and lacks nothing of value. She brings him good, not harm, all the days of her life (Prov. 31:10-12).

1. Meditate on this passage and write down observations. Look for key words, comparisons, contrasts, cause and effect, questions, and tone. Write down everything you find.

2. Write down a few principles you find in this passage.

   Do you see an application for you? What is it?

   The Book of Proverbs as a whole takes a view of marriage that remains proverbial to this day: that there is nothing in the world worse than a bad marriage, and at the same time nothing better than a good one (Mike Mason, *The Mystery of Marriage*, Multnomah, p. 24).

DAY 2
Women Who Bring Men Harm
Read Proverbs 31:1-3.

3. Using your imagination, describe the kind of woman who could "ruin a king" (or a man).

4. The following Proverbs warn about women who bring harm to their husbands and family. Describe each and give an example of how her behavior might dishonor her husband.

   2:16-17

12:4b

14:1

21:9

27:15

5. If you are a wife, how do you show your husband honor?

Action Assignment. Get a man's point of view. Ask a man whom you respect what kind of woman he thinks a man should avoid when choosing a wife. Then show him the above Proverbs. Ask him which one he would most severely warn his son against, if he had a son of marrying age. Record his comments below.

6. Did you learn anything from the Action Assignment? If so, what?

DAY 3
. . . .
Elizabeth, A Woman With a Clear Conscience
Sheila is a godly pastor's wife. At a bridal shower, she gave a devotional on getting along with your husband! Gently, she shared.

> Early on in our marriage my husband and I discovered that if there was trouble between us, there was usually something troubling our relationship with the Lord. So we would each get alone with the Lord and seek to clear up our relationship with Him. Then we found that our relationship with each other cleared up as well.

53

How I agree! And I believe that one of the reasons that the marriage of Zechariah and Elizabeth was so sound was because they each made sure their relationship with the Lord was good. For we are told:

> Together they lived honorably before God, careful in keeping to the ways of the commandments and enjoying a clear conscience before God (Luke 1:6, TM).

7. Describe the way a person must live in order to enjoy a clear conscience before God.

Do you agree that a clear conscience before God makes you a better wife? (a better friend?) Why or why not?

Read Luke 1:7.

8. Elizabeth had to live with the disappointment of barrenness, and yet she continued to love, trust, and obey God. Why do you think she responded that way?

I believe that Elizabeth knew God loved her. In your quiet time, sing the "Cares Chorus" (p. 104).

DAY 4 ....
Elizabeth, An Encouraging Life Partner
Read Luke 1:8-25. (In your group discussion, read aloud only verses 18, 24-25.)

9. Contrast the reactions of Elizabeth and Zechariah to Gabriel's news.

Elizabeth evidently had no problems in believing the fantastic promise, even though she had not received it as her husband had, directly from God through a godly messenger. . . . If Elizabeth did react more spiritually than her husband to the news, there is no evidence of any self-exaltation. Nor did she

54

look down on him. She didn't move him down in order to move herself up. Rather, she responded like a good wife who accepts weakness in her life-partner (Gien Karssen, *Her Name is Woman*, NavPress, p. 145).

10. Do you agree that it is important to accept weakness in your life-partner? Why or why not?

Read Luke 1:39-45.

11. What can you learn from Elizabeth's example of encouraging others spiritually?

How might a woman apply this to encouraging her husband spiritually?

DAY 5
Rebekah, Who With Her Own Hands, Destroyed Her Home

Rebekah was a believer and her marriage to Isaac began with great promise (Gen. 24). Yet, later in the marriage we see her tearing down her home with her own hands.

Read Genesis 27 on your own.

12. Summarize the events of the chapter in a few sentences.

13. List a few of the consequences of Rebekah's behavior for her marriage, her relationship with her sons, and their relationship with each other.

Rebekah failed to honor her husband, yet, as long as there is life, there is hope. Author and counselor Gary Smalley has said: "The secret to renewing any strained relationship is honor" (*If Only He Knew,* Zondervan, p. 4).

14. Rebekah's marriage to Isaac began with great hope as she trusted God. What do you think happened?

Do you find any warning for yourself in this story? If so, what?

PRAYER TIME

Pray in twos or conversationally, using your memory verse to guide you for part of your prayer time. Close by singing "Turn Your Eyes Upon Jesus" (p. 103).

Seven

She Finds Her Work to Be a Joy
The Idle Widows/The Diligent Widows

One of the most satisfying aspects of life is work! As a homemaker, I find it immensely gratifying to see my family enjoying a home-cooked meal around a candlelit table. As a writer, I love the creative process: praying, researching, seeing ideas take shape, working with words. As a co-laborer with other believers, seeing an evangelistic Bible study which I've helped plant take off and change lives is more exciting to me than a trip to a South Sea Island. This gives life meaning! Whether in the home, the workplace, or in ministry—work is a blessing! It was part of God's plan before the Fall and should be good. Even when it is menial, it can still be good, because it is part of my life's offering to God. If it is not satisfying, I need an attitude change!

WARMUP
Go around, giving women the freedom to pass, and ask: **Think about a recent time when your work in the home, or ministry, or the workplace gave you pleasure. What did you do and why did it give you joy?**

SCRIPTURE STUDY
DAY 1
. . . .
Attitude is Key
The Proverbs 31 woman whom Lemuel's mother urged him to find was talented, but what permeates the chapter is her attitude of

eagerness, of strength, of absolute delight in planning, executing, and enjoying the fruit of her labor.

Memorize the following:

> She watches over the affairs of her household and does not eat the bread of idleness (Prov. 31:27).

1. Meditate on the following verses describing the Proverbs 31 woman. What insight can you glean in each about her attitude? (In your personal quiet time, work thoughtfully through these verses.)

   v. 11

   v. 13

   v. 15

   v. 16

   v. 17

   v. 18

   v. 20

   v. 21

   v. 22

   v. 25

   v. 26

   v. 27

   v. 30

2. Summarize her attitude. What particularly impresses you?

Action Assignment. Is there a job in your home or workplace which needs to be done but you have been avoiding? Change your attitude and plan how and when you will accomplish it. What is your plan?

DAY 2
. . . .
The Secret of a Positive Attitude Toward Work
No matter what this 17th-century believer was doing, Brother Lawrence was offering it up to Christ, and his face radiated joy:

> The Special Diets kitchen was often very busy, and usually under-staffed. The phone seemed to ring incessantly . . . but, in the busiest moments, with noise, heat and tempers getting a bit frayed at the edges, Laurie remained calm—and close to God. . . . He was serving God, and that would be best done by being calm, composed . . . and hard-working (David Winter, *Closer Than A Brother*, Shaw, p. 160).

> Whatever you do, work at it with all your heart, as working for the Lord, not for men, since you know that you will receive an inheritance from the Lord as a reward. It is the Lord Christ you are serving (Col. 3:23-24).

3. Describe the attitude we should have according to the above passage.

The Christian attitude toward work is truly revolutionary. Think what it would do to the economy and the entire fabric of life if the question were asked daily, in the kitchen, in the office, the schoolroom, the plant: "Who is your Master?" and the answer were given: "Christ is my Master, whose slave I am" (Elisabeth Elliot, *Discipline: The Glad Surrender*, Revell, pp. 132–33).

4. If you fully realized that you were serving Christ in your work, how do you think it would impact your attitude toward:

Work that is menial and routine

Times when others do not notice your efforts

Your boss

Fellow employees

Your salary

DAY 3
She is Not Slothful
Sloth can simply be laziness: excessive sleeping, sitting around in front of the TV every evening, or finding excuses to escape work. It can also be substituting what we want to do for what God wants us to do.

5. What do you learn about the slothful person from the following word pictures or comparisons?

Prov. 6:6-11

Prov. 26:13-16

6. One Hebrew word which is translated *slothful* or *sluggard* has the connotation of deceit. What excuse does the lazy person give in Proverbs 22:13? What creative excuses have you given?

7. God says that the "heart is deceitful above all things and desperately wicked" (Jer. 17:9, KJV). Often we do not know that we are deceiving ourselves, and our excuses seem valid. Think

about some of the things God has called you to do but that you tend to avoid. What are those things?

In an article in *Leadership* (Spring 1994), John Ortberg points out that many lazy people are busy, for though sloth can be inactivity, it can also be "the failure to do what needs to be done when it needs to be done." God rejected Saul as king because Saul substituted activity for what God had called him to do (1 Sam. 15:1-23).

8. What jobs has God called you to do? How can you be sure you are not neglecting them?

9. The lazy person tends to be "wise in his own conceits" (Prov. 26:16), and yet he or she is really "void of understanding" (Prov. 24:30) for sloth leads to trouble. List the consequence of sloth in each of the following and explain how it could be hard in your life.

Prov. 10:26

Prov. 12:24

Prov. 13:4

Prov. 15:19

Prov. 20:13

Prov. 24:30-34

DAY 4
Idle Women
In his first letter to Timothy, Paul gives guidelines for deciding which widows in the church were worthy of support and which

were not. In part, these decisions were made on the basis of age and whether or not they had families, but also on the basis of whether their lifestyle was idle or diligent.

Review your memory verse.

As an overview, read 1 Timothy 5:3-16.
10. Describe the characteristics of the women who were wasting their lives according to verses 6 and 13.

11. Why is it that idleness often leads to gossip or being busybodies? What warning do you see here for yourself?

12. What do you think Paul means when he says she "is dead even when she lives"? (See also Revelation 3:1.)

In contrast, examine the following verse.

> I have been crucified with Christ and I no longer live, but Christ lives in me. The life I live in the body, I live by faith in the Son of God, who loved me and gave himself for me (Gal. 2:20).

13. In the above verse, what is the secret of a vibrant and meaningful life?

> One of the things that will happen to you when you give yourself to Jesus as Lord of your life is that He will give you the strength to serve Him (Tom Osborne, Coach of the Nebraska Huskers, FCA Banquet, 11/15/94).

In your personal quiet time, sing some of the songs found in the back of this guide.

DAY 5
Diligent Women
Paul commends the woman who "puts her hope in God and contin-ues night and day to pray and to ask God for help" (1 Tim. 5:5). Not only will these actions give a woman the strength to be dili-gent, but it will give her the wisdom to do what God is calling her to do.

14. How are women who led valuable lives described in 1 Timothy 5:9-10?

    Is God speaking to you through the above passage? If so, how?

15. What do you think you will remember about this lesson?

PRAYER TIME
Pray in twos or conversationally, using your memory verse to guide you for part of your prayer time. Close by singing the "Cares Chorus" (p. 104).

NEXT WEEK
If you have many young mothers in your group, divide Chapter 8 into two lessons, assigning Day 1 and Day 2 for next week.

Eight

She Trains Her Children
Herodias/Eunice and Lois

S usannah Wesley bore nineteen children and raised two
mighty men of God: John and Charles. Charles gave us some
of our most beloved hymns, including "Hark the Herald Angels Sing" and "Christ The Lord Has Risen Today!" Susannah
home-schooled her children and pulled her apron over her head for
her own devotional hour with the Lord. Before Susannah died,
John asked her to write down her philosophy of training young
children. She wrote:

> The children were always put into a regular method of living,
> in such things as they were capable of, from their birth; as
> in dressing, undressing, changing their linen . . . When
> turned a year old (and some before), they were taught to
> fear the rod and to cry softly; by which means they escaped
> abundance of correction they might otherwise have had; and
> that most odious noise of the crying of children was rarely
> heard in the house . . . They were never suffered to choose
> their meat, but always made to eat such things as were pro-
> vided for the family . . . In order to form the minds of chil-
> dren, the first thing to be done is to conquer their will and
> bring them to an obedient temper . . . The children of this
> family were taught, as soon as they could speak, the Lord's
> Prayer . . . and some portion of Scripture, as their memories
> could bear . . . They were quickly made to understand they

might have nothing they cried for and instructed to speak handsomely for what they wanted (*The Journal of John Wesley*, Moody, pp. 104–107).

WARMUP
Go around the circle, asking women to share one thing from Susannah Wesley's example that impresses them. As a review, ask volunteers to share their memory work of Proverbs 31:26-30.

SCRIPTURE STUDY
DAY 1
. . . .
Faithful Instruction Is On Her Tongue
Memorize the following passage.

> Her children arise and call her blessed; her husband also, and he praised her: "Many women do noble things, but you surpass them all" (Prov. 31:28-29).

1. John and Charles Wesley praised their mother, Susannah. What do you imagine were some of the qualities for which they were most thankful?

Read Deuteronomy 6:6-9.

2. What similarities do you see between this passage and Proverbs 31:26-27?

If you are a mother, how are you seizing opportunities to faithfully instruct your children?

Action Assignment. An often fatal mistake made by Christian parents is to delegate the discipling of their children to the church. Church activities are important, but God has called *parents* to disciple their children all through the day. If you have children at home, seize *at least* one opportunity *daily* to disciple your children. (Act out a Bible story, visit a shut-in, pray together, sing praises together, memorize and discuss a Proverb at dinner, etc.) Then list what you did.

DAY 2
. . . .
She Trains Her Children
To Respect and Obey Authority
Review your memory passage.

As a baby Christian with two little boys, I was a permissive mother who was reluctant to discipline. A Christian teacher called Steve and me in for a conference when our firstborn son went to school. Gently, this godly older woman told us:

> The happiest children are children who have been trained to respect authority. It's not too late for you to train your son. Go to him, ask his forgiveness, and tell him there will be a change. You and your husband must define the boundaries and paddle your son when he defies you. He will soon learn to respect you, the paddlings will become rare, and there will be hope for his future.

Today our three grown children are all walking closely with the Lord — in large part, I am convinced, because we helped them to respect and obey authority.

3. Read the following Proverbs and write down the principle which is being taught in each:

   Prov. 13:24

   Prov. 19:18

   Prov. 29:17

4. If you are an older mother and have experienced the truth of the above Proverbs, share something with the younger mothers to encourage them.

5. Based on the above Proverbs, what overriding principle do you see? Do you see an application for your life?

Many secular child psychologists are opposed to spanking, calling it child abuse. It is true that approaching a spanking in anger can be abusive. For this reason, as a young mom, I refused to spank. An author who helped me to see my error was Larry Christensen. *In The Christian Family* (Bethany), he explains that the world often spanks in anger, which is abusive, but a godly parent spanks with regret, to help his child learn to obey. Christensen says "the whole atmosphere is different and the children sense it at once."

Christensen also warns against provoking a child to wrath (Eph. 6:4). Don't, he warns:

(1) Punish them for childish irresponsibility (Dr. Dobson agrees—punish only for defiance).
(2) Set too many rules! Christensen says: "Many rules, many infractions."
(3) Elect a long, drawn out punishment (such as grounding them for a week).
(4) Allow them to show you disrespect (enforce the rules you've set down consistently).

As we put Christensen's wisdom into practice, our little boys became happier, more secure. They always preferred spankings to other forms of discipline—for then it was dealt with, and over. We hugged them, loved them, and put it in the past. Out of respect for their bodies, we found other forms of discipline in adolescence—though very little was needed.

Note: If you have many young mothers in your group and have decided to divide Chapter 8 into two lessons, you may want to stop here the first week.

DAY 3
. . . .
She Trains Through Positive Reinforcement

It is important to discipline disrespectful behavior. However, a mother who trains only through chastisement may discourage the spirit of her child and pave the way for future rebellion. Like sun and rain to a wilting flower are the words of praise and small rewards to a growing child.

> The wise in heart are called discerning, and pleasant words promote instruction (Prov. 16:21).

> Pleasant words are a honeycomb, sweet to the soul and healing to the bones (Prov. 16:24).

6. What do you learn from the above proverbs about pleasant words?

   Is there an application to your life?

Gifts, or, as it is sometimes translated, "bribes" can be used for evil or for good. When they are used to pervert justice, as in Proverbs 17:23, God condemns them. However, they can also be used to encourage good behavior. I agree with Dr. Dobson who encourages charts with stickers for good behavior such as a clean room, faithful practicing on the piano, well done chores, and reading good books. Those stickers eventually can be turned in for small prizes. I was always amazed at the power of stickers in helping children to develop good habits with a cheerful heart. My husband has said (in jest, I think) that he is going to put the following proverb on my tombstone, claiming it has been my life verse as a mother of five:

> A gift is as a precious stone in the eyes of him that hath it: whithersoever it turneth, it prospereth (Prov. 17:8, KJV).

7. What do you learn from the above proverb? Is there an application for your life?

Perhaps the most famous proverb concerning training children is Proverbs 22:6:

> Train a child in the way he should go, and when he is old he will not turn from it.

8. What principle is in the above verse? Is there an application for your life?

There has been much written by experts on the above proverb. Dr. John White in *Parents in Pain* reminds us that Proverbs are generalities, not promises. Therefore if you do all you can to raise a child to love the Lord, to respect authority, and to be a kind person — he probably will be, but there are exceptions, and good parents have been known to have rebellious children. Dr. James Dobson (*The New Dare to Discipline*) talks about the importance of understanding your child's particular bent ("the way he should go") and encouraging him in the way of his spiritual gifts, talents, and general strengths. Counselor Jay Adams (*Competent to Counsel*) has a different, but intriguing perspective on this verse. He feels it is a warning, rather than an encouragement. Literally, he says, it says "Train a child after the manner of his way" — in other words, if you train a child to believe he can have his own way, which is rebellious and foolish, when he is old, he will continue to want his own way, and not God's way. However, whether it is a warning or an encouragement, it is clear we are to train our children when they are young to love and serve God!

DAY 4
A Foolish Mother: Herodias
A Foolish Father: Eli
Read Mark 6:14-29. (In your group, read only verses 22-29.)
9. What do you learn about the character of Herodias from this passage?

69

10. How was Salome, her daughter, like her?

What negative attitudes might you be passing on to the next generation?

Read 1 Samuel 2:12-25.
11. Describe the behavior and attitude of Eli's sons.

Read 1 Samuel 2:27–3:14.
12. What prophecies were given to Eli? How did Eli fail as a father?

Why do you think Eli failed to restrain his sons when they were young? What are some reasons parents fail to restrain their children?

DAY 5 . . . .
Mothers Who Discipled Their Children: Lois and Eunice
Review your memory passage.

Read 2 Timothy 1:5.
13. What do you learn about Timothy? As you think over your life, would a child or grandchild watching you have seen times when you were trusting in God? If so, share one.

Read 2 Timothy 3:14-17.

14. What other things do you learn about Timothy's upbringing from this passage?

15. Practice explaining the Gospel (the Good News on how we can be forgiven and assured of heaven) so that a child could understand. (There's a visual explanation on pages 94–96.)

16. What have you learned about training your children that you think you will remember?

PRAYER TIME

Use Popcorn Prayer to lift up each woman. If she is a mother, pray particularly for her in that role. Close by singing the "Cares Chorus" (p. 104).

Nine

She Finds Favor

The woman of value is obedient to God because she loves and fears Him—and not to gain favor. Still, she is blessed. One of the prevailing themes of the Book of Proverbs is that blessings and honor abound on the righteous. This does not mean that we are free of trouble, but that God is with us in difficult times and blesses us in ways that those who don't obey Him can never know.

WARMUP

Go around, giving women the freedom to pass, and say: **Share a specific way God has blessed you as you have endeavored to trust and obey Him.**

SCRIPTURE STUDY
DAY 1
Her Works Endure

Perhaps the greatest blessing of all for a woman of value is the knowledge that her life will bear lasting fruit, for those things that are done for Christ endure forever. She is storing up treasures in heaven. In addition, her memory on earth is blessed, and her example is carried on from generation to generation.

Linda Barry, who grew up in poverty in a "disintegrating" family, watched her neighbor and learned from her. She says that, as a little girl, she loved going to Mrs. Taylor's house because "even if it wasn't happening in her house, just being near it counted for something." One day Linda sneaked over to Mrs. Taylor's at dawn:

> I stood on her porch knocking and knocking and knocking, weighing how much of a bother I was becoming against how badly I needed to see her. . . . When I told her my mom said I could eat with them, she laughed and pushed open the screen door. . . .
>
> I'll never forget that morning, sitting at their table eating eggs and toast, watching them talk to each other and smile. How Mr. Taylor made a joke and Mrs. Taylor laughed. How she put her hand on his shoulder as she poured coffee and he leaned his face down to kiss it.
>
> And that was all I needed to see. I only needed to see it once to be able to believe for the rest of my life that happiness between two people can exist.
>
> I vowed that I was going to grow up and be . . . just like Mrs. Taylor (*Newsweek,* special edition, Summer 1991).

1. Was there a "Mrs. Taylor" in your life, a woman whose example profoundly impacted you? If so, share briefly how she did.

Memorize the following:

> Give her the reward she has earned, and let her works bring her praise at the city gate (Prov. 31:31).

2. Read the following and explain how a godly woman's works endure. What impresses you?

> The memory of the righteous will be a blessing (Prov. 10:7a).
>
> A kindhearted woman gains respect (Prov. 11:16a).

For no one can lay any foundation other than the one that has been laid; that foundation is Jesus Christ. Now if anyone builds on the foundation with gold, silver, precious stones, wood, hay, straw—the work of each builder will become visible, for the Day will disclose it, because it will be revealed with fire, and the fire will test what sort of work each has done. If what has been built on the foundation survives, the builder will receive a reward. If the work is burned up, the builder will suffer loss; the builder will be saved, but only as through fire (1 Cor. 3:11-15, NRSVB).

DAY 2
She Finds Favor with God

Though the rain falls on the righteous and the unrighteous (Matt. 5:45), still, Scripture shows us that God gives special blessings to those who are faithful, who walk in integrity.

3. In the following verses, find the blessings that a woman walking in righteousness may experience. If you have experienced this blessing, share something about a specific time when you did:

   Prov. 1:32-33

   Prov. 3:3-10

   Prov. 3:33

   Prov. 15:29

   Prov. 28:13-14

4. Is there a blessing in your life for which you are particularly thankful right now? If so, what is it?

5. The Book of Proverbs also repeatedly makes the point that "the way of the unfaithful is hard" (Prov. 13:15b). What are some of the griefs that we may be spared if we do not harden our hearts? (Based on the above proverbs or your own observations.)

DAY 3 . . . .
She Finds Favor with Man
Though it is true that "everyone who wants to live a godly life in Christ Jesus will be persecuted" (2 Tim. 3:12), it is also true that many people will respect you, be at peace with you, and even show you favor.

6. In the following verses, discover how, and perhaps from whom, you may find favor if you walk in integrity.

   Prov. 11:24-25 (Compare to Luke 6:38)

   Prov. 16:7

   Prov. 31:28-29

7. How have you experienced blessings from others as you have lived for Jesus?

8. Proverbs repeatedly show that the wicked are despised by their fellowman. "The memory of the wicked will rot" (Prov. 10:7a). What are some of the reasons the wicked are despised by others? (Based on Proverbs or your own observation.)

DAY 4 . . . .
Jezebel, Out of Favor with God and Man
Queen Jezebel was an idolater, a liar, and a murderer. Her death was horrendously brutal and her memory, as Proverbs says will be

true of the wicked, is rotten. Her very name has become synonymous with evil.

9. What can you discover about Jezebel's wickedness from the following passages?

    1 Kings 16:29-33

    1 Kings 19:1-2

    1 Kings 21

    Proverbs 13:15a says "the way of the unfaithful is hard." Using your imagination, how do you think Jezebel's life might have been difficult?

10. Take a look at Jezebel's death.

    What prophecy did Elijah give concerning Jezebel's death in 1 Kings 21:23?

    Describe how Jezebel prepared to die in 2 Kings 9:30. What does this tell you about her heart?

    Describe her death in 2 Kings 9:31-37.

A faithful woman's example endures, as a sweet fragrance, but the example of the wicked is a stench. Jezebel's daughter Athaliah walked in her steps and murdered those in her way, even her own grandchildren (2 Kings 11:1).

DAY 5
Mary, Who Found Favor With God
Mary was honored above all women. As she realized, her memory would be precious, "all generations would call her blessed" (Luke

1:48). Would it not behoove us to study and emulate her? Two of Mary's many valuable attributes worth of emulation were her faith and her servant heart, as captured in the following poem by Lucy Shaw:

Too much to ask

it seemed too much to ask
of one small virgin
that she should stake shame
against the will of God.
all she had to hold to
were those soft, inward
flutterings
and the remember sting
of a brief junction — spirit
with flesh.
who would think it
more than a dream wish?
an implausible, laughable
defense.
and it seems much
too much to ask me
to be part of the
different thing —
God's shocking, unorthodox,
unheard of Thing
to further heaven's hopes
and summon God's glory.

Reprinted from *Polishing the Petoskey Stone*, by Luci Shaw, © 1990. Used by permission of Harold Shaw Publishers, Wheaton, IL 60189.

One characteristic of Mary was that she had a desire to praise God. Before you begin in your quiet time today, sing "For the Beauty of the Earth" (p. 102) and "Father, I Adore You" (p. 100).

Read Luke 1:26-38.

11. After reading the above passage, examine the following questions.

    A. How did Gabriel affirm Mary?

    B. Considering the risk, why do you think Mary responded to Gabriel as she did in verse 38?

    C. What risks is God asking you to take with your life? How are you responding?

Read Luke 1:39-48.

12. After reading the above passage, examine the following questions.

    A. Read verses 36 and 39. How is Mary responding to this news about Elizabeth? Why do you think she responds in this way?

    B. Share a time when God spoke to you through His Word or another person.

Read Luke 1:49-56.

13. Review verses 50, 52-53. Write down ways Mary saw those who were faithful experience favor from God.

14. Mary obviously was familiar with Scripture, committed it to heart, and pondered it. What do you learn about her from Luke 2:19?

As you ponder God's faithfulness to you in your heart, what are some of the incidents that stand out to you and what did you learn from them?

Action Assignment. Put a small box on your dining table with a notepad and pen. Whenever you are aware of God's faithfulness, record how and the date. Encourage family members to do likewise. At the end of the month, read and ponder them together.

15. As you reflect on Mary's life, what were some of the difficulties she faced? How do you see evidence of God's faithfulness and presence with her in those difficulties?

16. *The Living Bible* parapharases Proverbs 14:14 as "The backslider gets bored with himself; the godly man's life is exciting." Using your imagination, in what ways do you think Mary's life was exciting? And in what ways is your life exciting?

17. In what ways was and is Mary still being blessed for her faithfulness? Contrast this with Jezebel.

18. What do you expect to remember from this study?

PRAYER TIME
Close by singing "Father, I Adore You" (p. 100) in a round. Then pray in twos or conversationally, beginning with praise for God's faithfulness to you.

NEXT WEEK
Ask a few women to bring some paraphrases (such as *The Living Bible* or *The Message*) and other translations for next week's final review exercise.

Ten

Review

As Mary pondered the things from God in her heart, let us do likewise!

WARMUP
Go around, giving women the freedom to pass, and ask: **Of the Biblical women you've studied in this guide, who made the strongest impression on you? Why?**

SCRIPTURE STUDY
DAY 1
....

Her Heart (Lessons 1 and 2)
Review the following memory verses: Proverbs 31:30 and 4:23.

1. What has God impressed on your heart from the above memory verses?

2. What are some reasons a wise woman fears God?

3. How does fearing and loving God affect her life choices? Give some examples.

4. What are some ways a wise woman keeps her heart?

5. What do you remember about the following women? What will you learn from each?

Sapphira

The Hebrew Midwives

Mary of Bethany

Martha of Bethany

DAY 2 . . . .
She is Discreet (Lessons 3 and 4)
Review the following memory verses: Proverbs 31:26 and 11:22.

6. What has God impressed on your heart from the above memory verses?

7. Define *discretion*. Give a few examples.

8. Contrast a woman of discretion and a woman of indiscretion in regard to the use of her tongue.

9. What do you remember about the following women? What will you learn from each?

Euodia and Syntyche

Hannah

The Women of Zion in Isaiah 3

The Holy Women in 1 Peter 3

DAY 3
. . . .
She is Prudent and She Honors Her Husband
(Lessons 5 and 6)
Review the following memory verses: Proverbs 19:14 and 31:27.

10. What has God impressed on your heart from the above memory verses?

11. How is prudence similar to discretion? How is it different?

12. How did the following women exemplify prudence or the lack of it? What do you remember from each?

    Zeresh

    Abigail

13. How did the following women honor or dishonor their husbands? What can you learn from them?

    Elizabeth

    Rebekah

DAY 4
. . . .
She is Diligent and Trains Her Children
(Lessons 7 and 8)
Review the following memory verses: Proverbs 31:27-28.

14. What is God impressing on your heart from the above passage?

15. What do you remember from the following women? What did each teach you?

The idle widows of 1 Timothy 5

The diligent widows of 1 Timothy 5

Herodias

Lois and Eunice

DAY 5 ....
She Receives Favor From God and Man (Lesson 9)
Review the following memory verse: Proverbs 31:31.

16. What are some of the ways a woman living wholeheartedly for the Lord is blessed?

17. What did you learn from the lives of each of the following women?

Jezebel

Mary, the mother of Jesus

Final Review Exercise
In the discussion group, divide into circles of three or four women and do the following:

1. Have one women say a simple sentence prayer, asking God to open your eyes to what He wants to impress on your heart.
2. Have another woman read Proverbs 31:10-12, 26-31 in a different translation. Every woman should listen for a phrase that stands out to her.
3. Now have each woman share the phrase that stood out to her with no additional comments.

4. Have another woman read the same verses in a different translation, perhaps a paraphrase.
5. Now have each woman share, "I see" or "I hear."
6. Have another woman read the same verses in another translation.
7. Now have each woman share one way God is speaking to her
from this passage.
8. Now hold hands, and have each woman pray for the woman on
her right, asking God to help her obey what He has shown her
from this passage. If she cannot pray aloud, she can squeeze
her hand to show her she is praying silently.

Leader's Helps

YOUR ROLE:

A FACILITATOR FOR THE HOLY SPIRIT AND AN ENCOURAGER

A FACILITATOR FOR THE HOLY SPIRIT

People remember best what they articulate themselves, so your role is to encourage discussion and keep it on track. Here are some things you can do to help:

1. Ask questions and allow silences until someone speaks up. If the silence seems interminable, rephrase the question, but don't answer it yourself!
2. Direct the group members to look in the Scripture for their answers. For example, ask: "What verses show some of the difficulties in Penninah's life?"
3. Place chairs in as small a circle as possible. Space inhibits sharing.
4. Deal with the monopolizer:
   A. Pray not only for her control, but that you can help find ways to make her feel valued—for excessive talking often springs from deep emotional needs.
   B. Wait for her to take a breath and gently say: "Thanks, could we hear from someone else?"
   C. Go around the room with a question.
   D. Set down some ground rules at the beginning of the session. You can tell the group that you would like to hear from each person at least three times. So after they've spoken three times, they should give other group members a chance. You can even make a game of it and distribute pennies "to spend."
   E. Take the monopolizer aside and say: "You and I both share easily, but we have some women who are shy. How do you think we could help them to share more?"

5. The Action Assignments and memory work will be used mightily in your group members' lives. If they aren't doing these exercises, call a few from the group and ask them to be good examples with you. Soon the others will follow!

AN ENCOURAGER

Most women who drop out of a group do so not because the study is too challenging, but because they don't feel valued. As a leader, these are some of the things you can do to help each woman feel valued:

1. Greet each woman warmly when she walks in the door. This meeting should be the high point of her week!
2. Affirm answers when you can genuinely do so: "Good insight! Great! Thank you!" And always affirm nonverbally with your eyes, a smile, a nod.
3. If a woman gives a wrong or off-the-wall answer, be careful not to crush her. You can still affirm her by saying: "That's interesting—What does someone else think?" If you feel her response must be corrected, someone in the group will probably do it. If they don't, space your correction so it doesn't immediately follow her response and is not obviously directed at her.
4. If this is an interdenominational group, set this ground rule: No one is to speak unfavorably of another denomination.
5. Send notes to absentees and postcards to the faithful in appreciation.
6. Don't skimp on the prayer time. Women's emotional and spiritual needs are met during the prayer time, so allot one third of your time for that.

Leader's Helps for Chapter 1
She Loves and Fears God

Distribute the guides ahead of time and assign Chapter 1.

OPTIONAL DISCUSSION QUESTIONS
Circle the following questions to skip in discussion if you have a group that has trouble finishing on time: #5, #6, #13.

WARMUP
Bring name-tags and write the women's first names in large letters. You want the opening question about Charity to start the group off with a bang—so call on a few enthusiastic members.

SCRIPTURE STUDY
Helps for Specific Questions
Question #4. Be ready to share vulnerably yourself. Encourage many to share. This is also an opportunity to ask if anyone has been delivered from the fear of hell—and how.

Question #10. Scripture teaches both that wives should submit to their husbands (Eph. 5:22) and also that each of us will give an account to God (2 Cor. 5:10). When the two are in conflict, the historical model seems to be to obey God (Peter, Abigail). You might ask the group to give some examples of black-and-white issues where a woman would have to gently tell her husband she cannot do something.

Question #14. If time permits, hear from everyone.

Leader's Helps for Chapter 2

Her Heart Is Fully Devoted to Christ

OPTIONAL DISCUSSION QUESTIONS
Circle the following questions to skip in discussion if you have a group that has trouble finishing on time: #7, #8, #9.

SCRIPTURE STUDY
Helps for Specific Questions
Question #4. If you are confident everyone in your group understands the Plan of Salvation, you may skip this.

Question #10. Jesus was helping Martha to see that her attitude of self-pity was wrong and also affirming Mary for her devotion. Martha's phrase "don't you care" indicates her attitude.

PRAYER TIME
You may want to demonstrate conversational prayer for the group with three or four who will be able to show the importance of short prayers and praying by subject.

Leader's Helps for Chapter 3
She Speaks with Wisdom

Remember to bring pennies for the Action Assignment. Even if you do not have a monopolizer, this is a helpful assignment for the shy people, to encourage them to spend their pennies.

OPTIONAL DISCUSSION QUESTIONS
Circle the following questions to skip in discussion if you have a group that has trouble finishing on time: #2, #8, #10.

SCRIPTURE STUDY
Helps for Specific Questions
Question #2. If we are speaking insults, that is our nature. If we are also speaking praises, it is a cover-up, for you don't get both salt and fresh water from the same stream.

Question #9. Pave the way for honest sharing by giving an example of trouble you caused by poor use of your tongue.

She Is Discreet

OPTIONAL DISCUSSION QUESTIONS
Circle the following questions to skip in discussion if you have a group that has trouble finishing on time: #1, #7, #13.

SCRIPTURE STUDY
Helps for Specific Questions
Question #3. Peter says that husbands who are nonbelievers may be won without a word—however, this is not a prohibition against speaking of the Lord to an unsaved husband (See 1 Peter 3:15-16).

Question #6. Sarah called Abraham her lord. Today, a woman might show respect by taking his name in marriage, wearing a wedding ring, and never correcting him or speaking disparagingly of him in public. Your group can probably think of more!

PRAYER TIME
Demonstrate praying through Scripture with a friend before you send them off in pairs to do it.

She Is Prudent

OPTIONAL DISCUSSION QUESTIONS
Circle the following questions to skip in discussion if you have a group that has trouble finishing on time: #4, #5.

SCRIPTURE STUDY
Helps for Specific Questions
Action Assignment. I have found it helpful to prioritize with A's (must do), B's (should do), and C's (could do). I pray and make my list. Here's an example:

A-1 Quiet time
A-2 Shower and dress
A-3 Pick up house
A-4 Finish rough draft of Chapter 3
A-5 Pick up new neighbor and take her to Bible study
B-1 Calls: Dentist, Carol, and Mother
B-2 Vacuum
B-3 Write sympathy note to Mrs. Erickson
C-1 Walk with Jean

After discussion, you may decide to extend this Action Assignment into next week.

Question #13. Direct them to find ways in 1 Samuel 25:18, 23-26, 28.

She Honors Her Husband

WARMUP
Tell them not to worry about repetition, for God often uses repetition to bring home a point.

OPTIONAL DISCUSSION QUESTIONS
Circle the following questions to skip in discussion if you have a group that has trouble finishing on time: #8, #9.

SCRIPTURE STUDY
Helps for Specific Questions
Question #7. We all sin (1 John 1:10). It is what we do with that sin that determines whether or not we have a clear conscience (1 John 1:9).

Question #8. Evidences that Elizabeth spent time with God and therefore knew His character can be found in Luke 1:6, 24, 42-45.

Leader's Helps for Chapter 7

She Finds Her Work
to Be a Joy

OPTIONAL DISCUSSION QUESTIONS
Circle the following questions to skip in discussion if you have a group that has trouble finishing on time: #1, #4, #9.

SCRIPTURE STUDY
Helps for Specific Questions
Question #1. Ask: **What kind of attitude inspires confidence?**

Question #2. You may want to go around with this question, giving women the freedom to pass.

Question #10. Verse 13 talks about "going house to house." If time permits, you could ask when the use of the telephone becomes idleness.

Question #12. Spiritually dead.

Leader's Helps for Chapter 8
She Trains Her Children

If you have mothers with children at home, you may very well have difficulty finishing this in one lesson. I would suggest that instead of skipping questions, that you divide it into two weeks. Take the first two days the first week and the last three the second.

SCRIPTURE STUDY
Helps for Specific Questions
Question #10. "Like mother, like daughter" is taken from Ezekiel, and is actually used in a negative way. Surely that was true of Herodias and Salome!

Question #12. Often it seems easier to look the other way when your children disobey, but that's only short-term — it is far, far harder long-term.

EXPLAINING THE GOSPEL SO THAT
EVEN A CHILD COULD UNDERSTAND
Explain this during the study, using the following illustration.

1. Hold one hand up to represent God. God is holy (Isa. 6:3).

2. Drop the second hand far below the "Holy Hand" to represent the sinfulness of man. Man has fallen short of the holiness of God (Rom. 3:23).

3. God is just. He must punish sin (Rom. 3:25). Make a fist with the holy hand and hit the fallen hand.

4. But God is also merciful. Therefore He sent Jesus to die on a cross to take the punishment we deserve (Rom. 3:24). If we trust in Jesus, asking Him to be our Savior, God covers us with the righteousness of Christ. And though our sins may be as red as scarlet, now, when God looks down, they are as white as snow (Isa. 1:18). Show a white napkin covering the fallen hand.

5. However, if we do not trust in God's provision, then we are not covered. (Remove napkin) And God's wrath will hit us. Make a fist with the holy hand and hit the fallen hand (John 3:36).

Leader's Helps for Chapter 9
She Finds Favor

OPTIONAL DISCUSSION QUESTIONS
Circle the following questions to skip in discussion if you have a group that has trouble finishing on time: #1, #2, #10. You want to be sure you pace yourself to get to Mary—summarize Jezebel if you must, but don't skimp on Mary. Her model will inspire and lead to good sharing.

SCRIPTURE STUDY
Helps for Specific Questions
Question #9. Have them describe some of the emotions they see in Jezebel and how those kinds of emotions affect you. Also, describe Jezebel's reputation. How would they feel if that was their reputation?

Question #12A. Help them to see that Mary hurried. You might have them look at a map to see the distance between Nazareth and the hill country of Judea (outside of Jerusalem). Hopefully they will see that it was important to her to make this long trip because she was being sensitive to the Spirit's leading.

Question #12B. While God seldom speaks to us through angels, He does still speak to us. You might call on people if they look like they might have something to share!

Question #14. If time permits, go around with this one!

Review

OPTIONAL DISCUSSION QUESTIONS
When you have 20 minutes left, skip to the final review exercise.

FINAL REVIEW EXERCISE
This exercise, taken from "The African Model," is powerful. Remind the women to:

1. Pause and meditate before answering.
2. Use various Bibles, such as *The Living Bible* or *The Amplified Bible.*
3. Share only the phrase—*no* comment—in Step 3.

MEMORY VERSES

Chapter 1
Charm is deceptive, and beauty is fleeting; but a woman who fears the Lord is to be praised (Prov. 31:30).

Chapter 2
Keep thy heart with all diligence, for out of it are the issues of life (Prov. 4:23, KJV).

Chapter 3
She speaks with wisdom, and faithful instruction is on her tongue (Prov. 31:26).

Chapter 4
Like a gold ring in a pig's snout is a beautiful woman who shows no discretion (Prov. 11:22).

Chapter 5
Houses and wealth are inherited from parents, but a prudent wife is from the Lord (Prov. 19:14).

Chapter 6
A wife of noble character who can find? She is worth far more than rubies, Her husband has full confidence in her and lacks nothing of value. She brings him good, not harm, all the days of her life (Prov. 31:10-12).

Chapter 7
She watches over the affairs of her household and does not eat the bread of idleness (Prov. 31:27).

Chapter 8
Her children arise and call her blessed; her husband also, and he praises her: "Many women do noble things, but you surpass them all" (Prov. 31:28-29).

Chapter 9
Give her the reward she has earned, and let her works bring her praise at the city gate (Prov. 31:31).

Music

Closing with a song helps people leave a small group meeting with their focus on Jesus. Music Minister John Haines makes the following suggestions for a successful song time.

1. Teach the song the first time. Be sure you know it. If you cannot do this, delegate it to someone who can. Even if it is a familiar chorus to many, teach it the first time — for there will be those who don't know it.

2. Sing the song in a relatively low key.

© 1972 MARANATHA! MUSIC (Administered By THE COPYRIGHT COMPANY Nashville, TN) All Rights Reserved. International Copyright Secured. Used By Permission.

Doxology

Thomas Ken

Genevan Psalter, 1551;
attributed to Louis Bourgeois

Praise God from whom all bless-ings flow; Praise Him, all crea-tures here be-low; Praise Him a-bove, ye heav'n-ly host; Praise Fa-ther, Son and Ho-ly Ghost. A - men.

For the Beauty of the Earth

Folliott S. Pierpoint, altered

Conrad Kocher; arr. William H. Monk

1. For the beau-ty of the earth, For the glo-ry of the skies,
2. For the won-der of each hour Of the day and of the night,
3. For the joy of hu-man love, Bro-ther, sis-ter, par-ent, child;
4. For Thy Church that ev-er-more Lift-eth ho-ly hands a-bove,
5. For Thy-self, best gift di-vine, To our race so free-ly given;

For the love which from our birth O-ver and a-round us lies;
Hill and vale and tree and flower, Sun and moon and stars of light:
Friends on earth and friends a-bove; For all gen-tle thoughts and mild:
Off-ering up on ev-ery shore Her pure sac-ri-fice of love:
For that great, great love of Thine, Peace on earth and joy in heaven:

Lord of all, to Thee we raise This our hymn of grate-ful praise. A-men.

Turn Your Eyes Upon Jesus

Words and Music by
Helen Lemmel

Cares Chorus

Kelly Willard

I cast all my cares up-on You. I
lay all of my bur-dens down at Your feet. And
an-y time that I don't know what to do, I will
cast all my cares up-on You. I cast all of my
cares up-on You, I will cast all my

cares up-on You._____

poco rit.

Prayers and Praises

_____

_____

_____

_____

_____

_____

_____

_____

_____

_____

_____

_____

_____

_____

Prayers and Praises

Prayers and Praises

_____

_____

_____

_____

_____

_____

_____

_____

_____

_____

_____

_____

_____

Prayers and Praises

Prayers and Praises

Prayers and Praises

Prayers and Praises
